HOW WE FIND OTHER EARTHS

TECHNOLOGY AND STRATEGIES TO DETECT PLANETS SIMILAR TO OURS

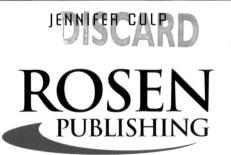

JENNIFER CULP

DISCARD

ROSEN PUBLISHING

NEW YORK

Published in 2016 by The Rosen Publishing Group, Inc.
29 East 21st Street, New York, NY 10010

Copyright © 2016 by The Rosen Publishing Group, Inc.

First Edition

Library of Congress Cataloging-in-Publication Data

Culp, Jennifer.
How we find other Earths / by Jennifer Culp.
p. cm. — (The search for other Earths)
Includes bibliographical references and index.
ISBN 978-1-4994-6292-0 (library binding)
1. Extrasolar planets — Juvenile literature. 2. Solar system — Juvenile literature. I. Culp, Jennifer, 1985-. II. Title.
QB820.C85 2016
523.2'4—d23

Manufactured in China

CONTENTS

INTRODUCTION

The universe is a fantastic and awe-inspiring place. Ever expanding and possibly infinite, it holds an unimaginable variety of matter—from the smallest subatomic particles to vast galaxies powered by the gravity of massive black holes. On Earth, we live in a unique solar system within the Milky Way galaxy, about 26,000–28,000 light-years from its center. Looking up into the night sky, we can see countless stars. Human beings have long suspected the existence of other worlds orbiting these stars, much as our own Earth takes its annual spin around the sun, but we had no way to detect these planets from our vantage point.

Until recently, that is. Astronomy and astrophysics advanced by leaps and bounds in the last two centuries. Between advances in actual scientific theory and in the sophisticated technology scientists and engineers are continually improving on, the detection and analysis of faraway

Thousands upon thousands of planets orbit stars in faraway solar systems. At present, we can detect only a tiny fraction of these planets from our position on Earth.

star systems transformed from fantasy into reality in the past several decades.

The term "exoplanet" is derived from the term "extrasolar," in which "extra-" refers to other stars or suns than our own. Thus, an exoplanet is a planet that revolves around another star than the one in our solar system, but it retains similarities to Earth.

Exoplanet science has exploded in the past twenty-five years since the first confirmed discovery of such a planet outside our own solar system. Before that, the existence of such planets was simply theoretical. According to the NASA Exoplanet Archive, we now know of 1,883 confirmed exoplanets, 472 multi-planet systems other than our own, and nearly 4,700 planetary candidates that have been discovered but still need to be verified by another means of detection. Improving technologies, including the development of both Earth-based and orbiting and other space satellite telescopes, is expected to expand the pool of possible candidates in the coming years.

The possibility of extraterrestrial life has been the subject of mythology, religion, and science fiction since human beings first started telling stories. Scientists around the world now work in collaboration to study exoplanets and hope to answer the question humanity has been asking for millenia: does life exist elsewhere in the universe?

CHAPTER ONE

WANDERING STARS: A HISTORY OF DISCOVERY

The people of planet Earth have known about other planets for a long, long time. Human beings have recognized five "classical" planets outside of our own Earth since ancient times. Venus, Mercury, Mars, Jupiter, and Saturn orbit close enough to Earth that they are occasionally visible to the naked eye. Ancient peoples who saw them in the night sky recognized these planets as "wanderers," and many thought that they were somehow related to the supernatural world. The names we still use for the planets of our solar system reflect this history: they are all named after Roman gods.

GEOCENTRIC VS. HELIOCENTRIC THEORIES

Early on, many observers on Earth assumed that the planets they saw actually rotated around Earth. Thinkers and scientists such as Claudius Ptolemy, who lived in Alexandria, Egypt, in the second century CE, believed in this model of the universe. Derived partially from the Greek word for Earth, "geo," this was the geocentric theory of rotation. Ptolemy, building on the work of even earlier investigators Apollonius of Perga and Hipparchus of Rhodes, wrote an entire astronomical treatise called the *Almagest* to explain the motions of the planets around Earth. As we know today, however, Ptolemy's ideas were incorrect.

Other scientists were on the right track about the true organization of the solar system even before Ptolemy's time, even though most of their contemporaries disagreed. As far back as 300 years before the Common Era—nearly 500 years before Ptolemy's time—Greek astronomer Aristarchus of Samos suspected that Earth

ad M B per-
pédicularis .
parallela igi-
tur eſt CM ip
ſi LX. eſt au-
tem & SX pa-
rallela ipſi M
R; ac propte-
rea triangu -
lum LXS ſi-
mile eſt trian
gulo M R C.
ergo vt S X
ad MR , ita S
L ad RC. ſed
S X ipſius M
R minor eſt,
quàm dupla;
quoniá & X
N eſt minor,
quàm dupla
ipſius MO. er
go & SL ip-
ſius CR mi-
nor erit, quã
dupla : &
R multo mi-
nor , quã du-
pla ipſius R
C. ex quibus
ſequitur S C
ipſius CR mi
noré eſſe, quã triplã. habebit igitur RC ad CS maio M

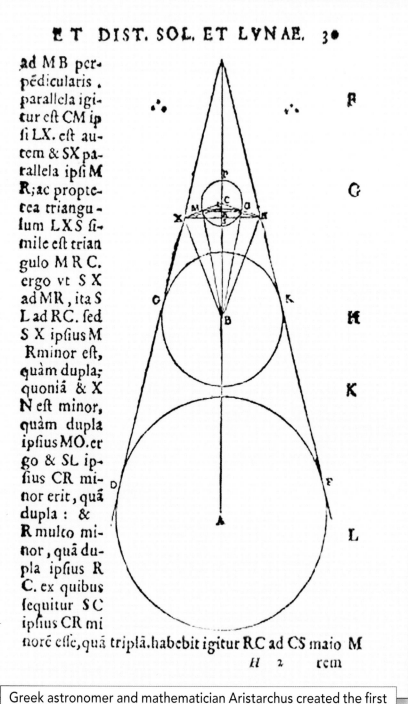

Greek astronomer and mathematician Aristarchus created the first known heliocentric model of the solar system, but his ideas were not widely accepted until thousands of years after his death.

was actually another planet rotating around the sun, and that stars were actually just far-distant suns similar to our own.

These ideas didn't gain widespread acceptance for nearly two thousand years, when Nicolaus Copernicus presented a mathematical model to prove that Earth orbited the sun in 1543. An early supporter of Copernicus's heliocentric (sun-centered) system named Giordano Bruno echoed Aristarchus's ideas, suggesting that distant stars are actually suns orbited by their own planetary bodies. Bruno even thought that these distant planets may contain life of their own . . . and was burned at the stake by the Roman Inquisition for this and other "heretical" beliefs in the year 1600.

"WANDERERS" AND PLANETS

The following century saw greater understanding of the local planets and their movements, however. Italian scientist Galileo Galilei, upon hearing of the invention of the telescope, built one of his own and aimed it upward to observe the "wanderers." Using information provided by Galilei's observations, German mathematician and astronomer Johannes Kepler was able to uncover and explain three scientific laws of planetary motion, greatly improving human understanding of our own solar system.

As telescopes were used more widely and became more powerful, the number of "planets" shot up as astronomers continually spotted new bodies in the night sky. In the mid-1800s,

Unlike Aristarchus's heliocentric model of the solar system, Hipparchus of Rhodes explained how the planets, the moon, and the sun all circle Earth. His ideas would later be proven incorrect.

scientists realized that some of the new planets were actually objects that were quite different from the classic wanderers of old. Because Saturn (discovered in 1781) and Neptune (discovered in 1846) were so much larger than the other new "planets," they retained planetary status while other objects (including Ceres, which is now classified as a dwarf planet) were reclassified as asteroids.

ROGUE PLANETS

Exoplanets orbit around stars the way Earth rotates around the sun. These aren't the only planetary-mass objects that exist in space, however—rogue planets orbit the galaxy itself, rather than a stellar body. A rogue planet may have been ejected from the planetary system in which it originally formed, or it may have never been gravitationally bound to a star at all. These rogue planets, which are thought to have formed in the same manner as stars, are referred to as sub-brown dwarfs by the International Astronomical Union to distinguish them from exoplanets that orbit stars.

WHAT MAKES A PLANET A PLANET?

In the twentieth century, the discovery of Pluto and its subsequent classification as a planet set off a firestorm of controversy and led to further restructuring and a new definition of what counts as a planet—inside the bounds of our own solar system, that is. In 2006, the International Astronomical Union finally managed to pass a resolution to define officially what constitutes a planet in our solar system. Within our solar system, a "planet" is defined as: "A celestial body that (a) is in orbit around the Sun, (b) has sufficient mass for its self-gravity to overcome rigid body forces so that it assumes a hydrostatic equilibrium (nearly round) shape, and (c) has cleared the neighborhood around its orbit."

In simpler terms, a planet must revolve around the sun, have a high enough mass that its gravity forces it into a round shape (but not so much mass that it triggers nuclear fusion in its core and becomes a star!), and have a high enough mass that its gravity sucks in almost all wayward space debris (such as asteroids) that cross its orbital path. This definition situated Earth-dwellers in a solar system–wide "neighborhood" of eight planets—Mercury, Venus, Earth, Mars, Jupiter, Saturn, Uranus, and Neptune. (Pluto, which was considered to be a planet from 1930 to 2006, is now classified as a "dwarf planet" along with Ceres, Eris, Haumea, and

Clyde Tombaugh discovered Pluto in 1930 by monitoring the skies with a telescope housed in the Lowell Observatory in Flagstaff, Arizona.

Makemake.) This definition applies only to the planets of our own local solar system, however. By the time astronomers managed to agree on a definition for planetary bodies that orbit within our solar system, they had already been working to formulate a working definition for planets in other parts of the galaxy.

EARLY SEARCHES FOR OTHER EARTHS

This was far from the first time anyone had claimed to find evidence of an exoplanet. A binary star system about 16.6 light-years away from Earth, 70 Ophiuchi, tricked several would-be exoplanet discoverers. (A binary star system contains two stars that orbit around a common center of mass, revolving around one another. To the unaided human eye, 70 Ophiuchi appears as a single dim star.)

In 1855, Captain W. S. Jacob claimed to have discovered an orbital anomaly within the system. Reasoning that the pull from gravity of an unseen body must be responsible for the anomaly within 70 Ophiuchi's orbital pattern, Jacob believed he had discovered an extrasolar planet. "We may suppose a third body to belong to the system, and to be opaque, and

A rogue planet, such as the one depicted in this artwork, may owe its orphan status to interaction with a giant planet whose gravity threw the smaller rogue out of orbit.

consequently invisible; such a body would, of course, disturb the regularity of the motions of the other two," he wrote in a report for the *Monthly Notices of the Royal Astronomical Society*.

In 1943, astronomers Dirk Reuyl and Erik Holberg published "On the Existence of a Third Component in the System 70 Ophiuchi" in *The Astrophysical Journal*, claiming that the mysterious "third body" was one-tenth the mass of our sun. Both of these claims—along with others of

This artwork shows how gravity affects orbiting stars: the more powerful magnetic field of the larger white dwarf star (in red) pulls atmospheric matter away from the smaller brown dwarf (blue).

their kind—were shown to be incorrect.

But not every exoplanet discovery made during this earlier era was a false alarm. In 1989, Canadian astronomers Bruce Campbell, G. A. H. Walker, and Stephenson Yang located what appeared to be a planet in the Gamma Cephei system. However, the discovery stretched the very limits of technological capability at the time, casting doubt on the legitimacy of the find. To add to the confusion, the astronomers were mistaken about the size of the star the planet orbited, giving a misleading impression of its mass and the newly suspected planet's mass.

No extrasolar planet had been officially identified and confirmed at the time, and other scientists remained skeptical of the discovery. Only fifteen years later would their achievement of the very first exoplanet discovery be verified, when improvements in radial velocity technique (which we'll discuss in more detail in chapter 3) confirmed the presence of a Jupiter-mass planet orbiting one of the stars in the binary Gamma Cephei system.

CHAPTER TWO

BEYOND THE SOLAR SYSTEM

T he modern era has been marked by dramatic advances in space observation and exploration. Often, scientists investigating one phenomenon can inadvertently uncover the existence of other, unexpected ones. The search for exoplanets had some of its most exciting discoveries toward the end of the twentieth century.

"THREE FIRSTS"

In 1990, radio astronomers Aleksander Wolszczan and Dale Frail were working at the Arecibo Observatory in Arecibo, Puerto Rico, when they discovered the pulsar star PSR B1257+12, over one thousand light-years from our solar system's

The Arecibo Observatory in Puerto Rico is home to the world's largest single-aperture radio telescope, which has been used to gather data for many extraterrestrial research projects.

sun. Pulsars are types of neutron stars, which are very dense stars that can result from the collapse of a massive star, and are the smallest and densest stars in the universe. Pulsars are highly magnetized and spin rapidly, and produce one or more beams of radiation. These beams of radiation sweep past Earth like a searchlight, and are known as a pulse, hence the naming convention. Wolszczan and Frail noticed that there were odd differences, or anomalies, in the pulsation period for this particular pulsar. They began trying to uncover the cause or causes of these anomalies.

Their investigation led to Wolszczan and Frail announcing an incredible discovery in 1992: they had located two planets orbiting PSR B1257+12. With this discovery, Wolszczan and Frail confirmed the existence of what ancient astronomers had merely suspected: exoplanets, planets that orbit stellar bodies other than our familiar sun, in their own far-away solar systems.

A mere four years after Campbell, Walker, and Yang's contested discovery, Wolszczan and Frail had utilized the same technique in their pioneering work. With this discovery, Wolszczan and Frail "had bagged three firsts," as David Stevenson recounts in the book *Under a Crimson Sun*: "the first confirmed extrasolar planets, the first multi-planet system, and finally the first super-terrans—planets with only marginally more mass than Earth." A third planet was confirmed in 1994.

DEFINING EXOPLANETS

In 1995, Michel Mayor and Didier Queloz

Michel Mayor (pictured here in 2007) and Didier Queloz made the first discovery of an exoplanet orbiting a main-sequence star in 1995.

detected an exoplanet orbiting the star 51 Pegasi, which is a main-sequence star (or "dwarf" star) like our own sun. By the turn of the twenty-first century, the International Astronomical Union had come up with some temporary criteria to determine what does and doesn't count as an exoplanet. A planet can't be too big or too small. Above a mass of about thirteen Jupiters put together, a celestial object becomes so big that thermonuclear fusion reactions of the element deuterium can take place within its core. Space objects of or above this size are considered to be brown dwarf stars, rather than planets.

However, like planets within our solar system, any object that is considered a planet must be big enough to maintain a round shape and clear its orbit of debris. In order to qualify as a planet, an object must orbit a star or stellar remnant (that is, an old dead star). Free-floating planet-sized objects that do not orbit a star or stellar system are called "sub-brown dwarfs." In summary: an object that revolves around a star that is big enough to clear its

HOW EXOPLANETS GET THEIR NAMES

Exoplanets are catalogued with a seemingly simple—but often confusing to the layperson—system. According to the International Astronomical Union, "The scientific nomenclature for the designations of exoplanets usually consists of two elements: 1) a proper noun or abbreviation, sometimes with associated numbers 2) followed by a lowercase letter. The first element can derive from a number of sources. A common source is an exoplanet's host star's widely recognized, common or astronomical catalogue name. Alternatively, exoplanets are often named after the scientific instrument or project that discovered the exoplanet." For example, the planet 51 Pegasi b revolves around the star 51 Pegasi.

The process for choosing popular names for exoplanets is organized by the IAU "Public Naming of Planets and Planetary Satellites" working group. Acceptable proposals include names that are sixteen characters or less in length, preferably one word, pronounceable, non-offensive, and not too similar to a pre-existing name of an astronomical object. Unfortunately, the IAU specifically prohibits naming an exoplanet after a pet animal.

orbit but small enough that it can't fuse deuterium in its core is currently defined as a planet. As the Working Group on Extrasolar Planets of the International Astronomical Union pointed out when they released these criteria in 2003, however, this definition is not intended to be set in stone. "We can expect this definition to evolve," the group members stated, "as our knowledge improves."

Throughout the course of the next decade, astronomers identified other exoplanets, but, due to the limitations of research methods, these planets were almost all one of three types: gas giants (like our own Jupiter, though they can be much larger), ice giants (such as Uranus and Neptune), and super-Earths (which have a mass higher than Earth's but smaller than that of Uranus, which is about fifteen Earth masses).

NEW DISCOVERIES IN THE 21ST CENTURY

In 2009, NASA launched the Kepler space observatory (named for seventeenth-century

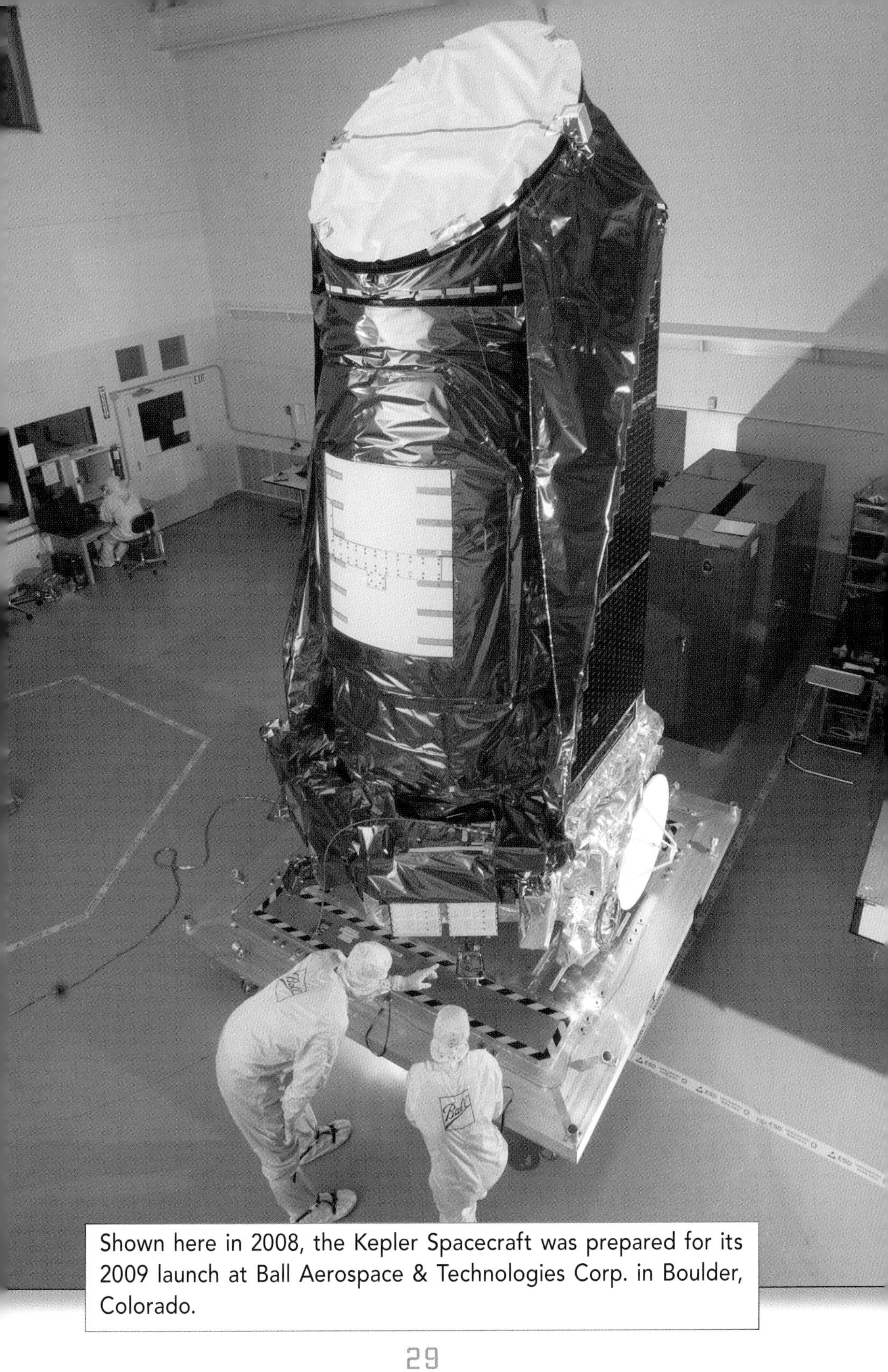

Shown here in 2008, the Kepler Spacecraft was prepared for its 2009 launch at Ball Aerospace & Technologies Corp. in Boulder, Colorado.

scientist Johannes Kepler) in an attempt to discover Earth-like terrestrial planets, "especially those in the habitable zone of their stars where liquid water and possibly life might exist." This "habitable zone," also known as the "Goldilocks zone," means the planet must be close enough to its star that the water is frozen into ice, but far enough away that the temperature remains in liquid form rather than becoming heated into steam.

In December 2011, astronomers working on the Kepler mission made an exciting announcement: Kepler had discovered two planets—one about the same size as Earth, and the other slightly smaller than Venus—orbiting a far-distant star. Both of these planets (termed "Kepler 20e" and "Kepler 20f") orbited far too close to their star to fall within the Goldilocks zone of their system (Kepler 20e, the smaller and closer planet, has a temperature of about 1,400 degrees Fahrenheit (760 degrees Celsius) at a distance of 5 million miles (about 8 million kilometers) from its star, which is slightly smaller and cooler than our own sun). They were, however, by far the smallest exoplanets humans had managed to locate and confirm yet. Kepler team member Geoffrey Marcy called the discovery "a watershed moment in human history." As reporter Dennis Overbye wrote of the discovery in the *New York Times*, the location of Kepler 20e and Kepler 20f "was an encouraging sign that planet hunters would someday succeed in the goal of finding Earth-like abodes in the heavens."

Originally the Kepler mission was intended to last for 3.5 years, from 2009 to mid-2012, but the mission was extended in order to fulfill all mission goals. In 2013, however, equipment failure put the mission in jeopardy. At this point, Kepler had identified more than 3,500 planetary candidates, more than 100 of which had been validated by another detection method, and the Kepler team wasn't ready to give up yet. In order to continue, NASA had to change the plan. Before the year was out, the K2 Second Light mission plan was approved. The new plan, which would utilize Kepler's remaining capability in order to study "supernova

In 2012, NASA extended the Kepler Observatory's K2 mission through 2016, four more years to search for alien planets than originally planned.

© D. van Ravenswaay

explosions, star formation and solar-system bodies such as asteroids and comets" in addition to searching for exoplanets, according to the mission statement, was initiated in 2014.

In December 2013, NASA announced the first verified exoplanet discovered by K2 (which was located accidentally while the spacecraft was being prepared for the full mission): a super-Earth called HIP 116454 b. As of mid-2015, the Kepler mission had identified 4,661 exoplanet candidates, 1,028 of which have been confirmed, and K2 has located 22 confirmed exoplanets. Of this number,

11 "small" near-Earth-sized planets within the Goldilocks zones of their respective stars have been located, and the search continues.

GPI AND DIRECT IMAGING

In the second decade of the twenty-first century, technology took another leap forward with the creation and implementation of the Gemini Planet Imager, or "GPI" for short. GPI actually locates exoplanets by direct imaging, a technique that was previously impossible due to the disparity in the tiny amount of light reflected by a planet in comparison to the amount of light produced by its host star. The Gemini Planet Imager is a very powerful high-contrast imaging instrument that can actually suppress the brightness of a star enough to allow for visible detection of any planets in the surrounding system. GPI is sensitive enough to detect the light of a planet itself in order to determine its mass and composition, and spectroscopic information provided by GPI's direct imaging helps researchers learn about the planet's size,

A distant super-Earth is seen from the point of view of the surface of its moon in this artwork. Another planet can be seen transiting across the surface of the system's host star in the background.

temperature, gravity, and even the composition of its atmosphere. "Most planets that we know about to date are only known because of indirect methods that tell us a planet is there, a bit about its orbit and mass, but not much else," explained Bruce Macintosh (leader of the team that built the instrument) in a 2014 press release. "With GPI, we directly image planets around stars—it's a bit like being able to dissect the system and really dive into the planet's atmospheric makeup and characteristics."

The creation of GPI required the combined effort of many people. The Gemini Planet Imager was funded by an international partnership, including the United States, the United Kingdom, Canada, Australia, Argentina, Brazil, and Chile—and built in a collaborative effort by institutions in the US and Canada, including the American Museum of Natural History, Dunlap Institute, Gemini Observatory, Herzberg Institute of Astrophysics, Jet Propulsion Laboratory, Lawrence Livermore National Lab, Lowell Observatory, SETI Institute, the Space Telescope Science

The interior of the Southern Gemini Telescope in Chile. With its sibling Gemini North in Hawaii, the two telescopes provide near-complete coverage of the skies (besides small regions around Earth's poles).

Institute, the University of Montreal, the University of California at Berkeley, the University of California at Los Angeles, the University of California at Santa Cruz, and the University of Georgia.

After five years of development, the instrument was installed at Gemini South, a telescope in the Andes Mountain Range in Chile. GPI had its first light (the first time a new telescope or new instrument is used to take an astronomical image) in November 2013. During its first week of operations, GPI imaged three planets in a known system, revealing that two of the planets that were previously thought to be similar in size and composition might be very different. In 2014, GPI entered full operational status and began a survey of 600 selected stars thought to be likely hosts for young gas giants, the type of planets GPI is best at imaging. Today, scientists from each country represented in the Gemini Community use GPI to examine distant planetary systems.

As of January 2015, more than twenty exoplanets had been detected by direct imaging (not including brown dwarves), and many more will be surveyed in years to come. A month after GPI's first light, the European Southern Observatory successfully tested SPHERE—which stands for Spectro-Polarimetric High-contrast Exoplanet Research instrument. SPHERE was then reassembled to begin its hunt for exoplanets on the Very Large Telescope at Paranal

Four telescopes work together to form the Very Large Telescope in Chile. With their data combined, these instruments can obtain a resolution high enough to directly observe a man on the moon.

Observatory in Chile in spring 2014. The current roster of direct imaging instruments is rounded out by the National Astronomical Observatory of Japan's Subaru Coronagraphic Extreme Adaptive Optics system (SCExAO), located at the Mauna Kea Observatory in Hawaii.

TESS, EVRYSCOPE, AND PLATO

In 2017, NASA plans to launch the Transiting Exoplanet Survey Satellite (TESS) in order to search for planets orbiting nearby stars using the same search technique utilized by Kepler. The European Southern Observatory has already announced first light for the Next-Generation Transit Survey, a twelve-telescope array that will monitor neighboring stars from the surface of Earth in Chile. Both of these projects aim to gather data on exoplanets revolving around stars closer to Earth than those surveyed in the Kepler mission.

A new instrument known as Evryscope began operating at the Cerro Tololo Inter-American Observatory in Chile in May 2015.

Evryscope, which monitors a wider field than any other exoplanet-detecting instrument built to date, will search for gas giants orbiting far-away stars and Earth-like planets revolving around nearby dwarf stars.

In 2024, the European Space Agency plans to launch a space-based observatory to search for exoplanets in the PLATO mission: PLAnetary Transits and Oscillations of Stars. From its position in orbit, PLATO will be able to search for planets around close to a million stars spread across half of the sky. PLATO will also investigate seismic activity in the stars themselves, allowing for measurement of the mass, radius, and age of each host sun. The PLATO mission will survey thousands of faraway planetary systems, but it will focus on discovering and describing Earth-sized planets in the habitable zones of their parent stars.

The examples listed here are only a few of the exoplanet discovery and research projects currently underway worldwide. According to the *Extrasolar Planets Encyclopaedia*, there are seventy-one ongoing and planned ground-based exoplanet observation programs as of summer 2015, plus twenty-one space-based exoplanet observatories. Each of these projects continues to make exciting discoveries, and fresh exoplanet news appears in the media nearly every week. In late 2013, NASA published a thirty-year strategic roadmap report and identified three main science goals (or "quests," as NASA's Aki Roberge describes them) for exoplanet science in the next three decades. Its first aim is to catalogue the "exoplanet zoo" and the basic properties of the exoplanets. Secondly, NASA aims to better characterize the discovered planets in detail. The mission's third aim is to begin the search for life on alien worlds.

CHAPTER THREE

HOW TO SEARCH FOR OTHER WORLDS

Between 1992 and 2015, more than 1,800 confirmed exoplanets have been identified outside of our solar system. But how are they identified? The major obstacle to research of exoplanets is distance. Planets in other solar systems are so, so far away from observers on Earth that—from our perspective—they are very difficult to detect. They are much too far away to be seen through a normal telescope, and even in the case of very high-powered telescopes that can spot far-off stars, the light reflected from planets is so little in comparison to that of their parent stars that they are rendered invisible. How, exactly, do exoplanet searchers reach across those vast distances to find alien planets?

USING DOPPLER SPECTROSCOPY

The first confirmed discoveries of exoplanets—the initial pulsar-orbiting planets located by Aleksander Wolszczan and Dale Frail in 1992, and Campbell, Walker, and Yang's earlier discovery of a planet orbiting Gamma Cephei, but confirmed later— were achieved through indirect radial velocity observations, also known as Doppler spectroscopy. According to the Planetary Society, the radial velocity method is the most effective method of locating exoplanets to date. This method uses measurements of a star's

This artwork depicts the shining pulsar star PSR B1257+12 and the three planets Alexander Wolszczan discovered orbiting it in 1992. The nearest planet is crowned with a halo-like aurora.

movements slightly toward and away from Earth to detect the presence of exoplanets.

When a planet orbits a star, the star doesn't just hold still in space while the planet revolves around it. Even though the star is enormously bigger than the planet, the planet exerts a small gravitational pull on the star, causing it to move slightly in response to the movement of the planet. On Earth, instruments called spectrographs can measure a faraway star's light spectrum with a high degree of detail. A star's normal light spectrum, or color signature, changes slightly as the star moves toward and away from Earth, shifting toward the blue end of the spectrum as it moves toward the observer and toward the red end of the spectrum as it moves away. As the far-off planet revolves around the star and causes it to move slightly toward and away from Earth, planet hunters here on our planet will detect regular shifts in the star's spectrum, moving regularly from red, to blue, and back again. The radial velocity method can tell observers whether or not a star is orbited by a body or bodies with near-certainty, and it is an effective method for detecting exoplanets from the surface of Earth, according to the Planetary Society. However, there are some drawbacks to Doppler spectroscopy.

The main problem with the radial velocity method is that it does not provide the mass of the object orbiting the star and causing the spectral shift. This is significant because, as mentioned earlier, if a celestial body is bigger than thirteen Jupiter masses, it no longer qualifies as a planet. At that size, it is classified as a brown dwarf star. The radial velocity method can only provide an estimate of the detected body's minimum mass, and some of the "planets" discovered using spectroscopy might actually be low-mass stars.

Additionally, radial velocity might miss completely the presence of a planet affecting the movement of its parent star. This is because shifts in the star's color signature only become apparent to spectrographs when the star moves toward and away from Earth. If the distant planetary system appears "edge-on" (as the Planetary Society puts it) to Earth, so that the orbiting body travels between its star and Earth each time it revolves around the star, Doppler spectroscopy will detect shifts in the star's spectrum and recognize the presence of the orbiting body.

But if the far-off planetary system is lined up perpendicularly to an Earth observer, this is another story. Imagine the system is laid out "face on" to Earth, where—if we could see it— the star sits at the center of a huge imaginary clock face, and the bodies orbiting it move around it like the hands of a clock without ever crossing between the star and Earth. The star would still move slightly in response to the planet's orbit, but it would appear to wiggle side-to-side instead of moving slightly toward and away. In this case, radial velocity would detect no change in the star's light spectrum and remain blind to the presence of any planet or orbiting body in the system.

Precise radial velocity measurements have still contributed immensely to the ongoing exoplanet hunt. Instruments such as the High Accuracy Radial velocity Planetary Search project (HARPS) continue to utilize the radial

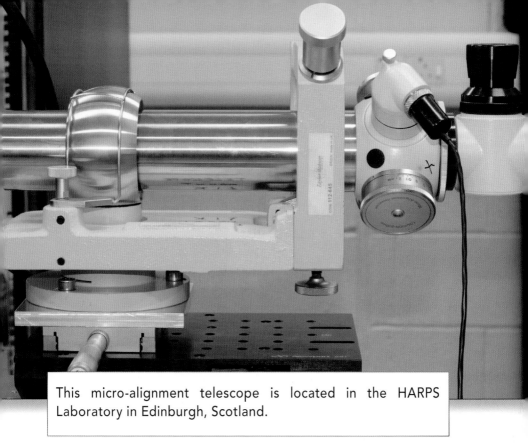

This micro-alignment telescope is located in the HARPS Laboratory in Edinburgh, Scotland.

velocity method to search for super-Earths and low-mass giant planets.

TRANSIT PHOTOMETRY

Another successful indirect method of locating exoplanets is called transit photometry. Like the radial velocity method, this technique depends on the planet passing between the light of its parent star and Earth as it orbits. This passage of a planet between an alien star and Earth is known as a "transit." When a planet transits across the face of its star, it blocks out a tiny bit of the star's light to an observer on Earth. This periodic dimming of the star's light as the planet regularly crosses between the star and Earth as it orbits lets observers know that a planet is likely present in the system. The amount of starlight blocked by a planet's transit is directly proportionate to the planet's size. Since a star's size can be measured with a high degree of accuracy, transit photometry can thus provide researchers with a good estimation of a planet's size by measuring how much light the

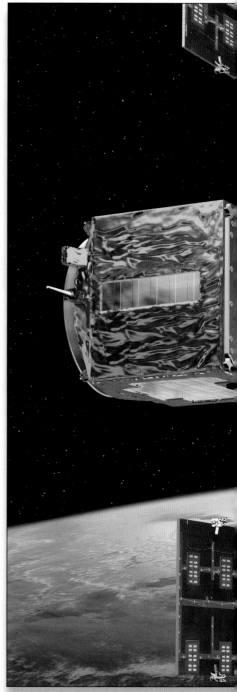

This artist's rendering shows the interior layout of the French COROT satellite, which was launched on a mission to search for exoplanets in 2006.

planet blocks when it transits across the face of the star.

Transits also provide information about the composition of a planet's atmosphere by measuring the way it absorbs different wavelengths of light as it passes the star. The amount and type of light absorbed by the gasses of the planet's atmosphere tells scientists which gasses are present in the atmosphere. "Secondary" transits—when a planet passes "behind" the star (from our perspective) and is completely invisible from Earth's vantage—help observers identify the planet's spectrum with further accuracy, even allowing for determination of the planet's temperature.

The transit method can determine planetary size effectively, but it can't offer planet hunters any valuable information about the planet's mass. (Mass and size are different measurements. Size is a measurement of how large an object is in volume—that is, how much space it takes up. Mass is basically a measurement of how much matter is packed into the space the object takes up. A large gaseous planet might be less massive than a smaller rocky planet, for example, because it is composed of spread-out particles of gas rather than tightly-packed particles of solid rock.)

The radial velocity method, as we discussed earlier, cannot determine the size of an orbiting body but can make an estimation of its minimum mass. Transit photometry can provide an accurate estimate of the body's size, but it cannot calculate its mass. When the two methods are combined, however, they can provide a very good estimation of the object's size, mass, and density—vital clues when it comes to determining the planet's composition. Combined transit and radial velocity data provide such an accurate picture because when a planet transits, it is always in the ideal "edge-on" alignment with Earth that allows for the most accurate possible data obtained through radial velocity measurements. "Under these conditions, the minimum mass normally provided by radial velocity measurements is, in fact, the planet's true mass," the Planetary Society's website explains.

This artwork depicts one of the two exoplanets discovered by Wolszczan and Frail in 1992 orbiting the pulsar star PSR B1257+12.

With all of this infor-
mation, scientists can
deduce the planet's mass,
size, temperature, atmo-
spheric composition, den-
sity, and possibly even
make assessments as to
the materials the planet
itself is composed from.
This combined approach
allows for confirmation of
planetary status, allowing
planetary "candidates" to
become verified as official
exoplanets. There is still a
big disadvantage to the
transit method, however.
For it to work, a transit
must occur. If the plane-
tary system is not lined
up precisely "edge-on"
to the observer, no transit
can be detected at all, and
no data can be obtained

from transit photometry. Furthermore, even when a system is lined up perfectly, a transit still only lasts for a very small fraction of the planet's total orbital period. Without constant monitoring, observers are unlikely to view a transit in progress, and astronomers must observe repeated regularly occurring transits in order to successfully identify and observe an exoplanet using this method.

KEPLER: SPACE-BASED TRANSIT PHOTOMETRY

Kepler, the space-based observatory, has provided scientists a solution to these problems. Kepler uses transit photometry in order to find exoplanets. The spacecraft follows Earth around the sun, keeping its photometer pointed continuously at a single star-field containing about 145,000 stars. Very few of those stars are undergoing a transit at any one time, but because Kepler's sensitive photometry instrument can monitor such a huge number of stars, it still obtains thousands of results.

Kepler was equipped with four reaction wheels to keep its photometer pointed in the right direction, but by 2013 two of the wheels failed, putting the mission in jeopardy. Fortunately, the Kepler team devised a plan to stabilize the position of the observatory by utilizing the pressure exerted by photons of sunlight as a sort of "third wheel" in order to keep the craft stable and balanced. To date, the Kepler mission and subsequent K2 Second Light mission have successfully identified more exoplanet candidates and confirmed exoplanets through transit photometry than any other method of exoplanet hunting so far.

NaCo

The very first exoplanet viewed by direct imaging is a gas giant about five times larger than Jupiter that orbits a brown dwarf about 230 light-years away from Earth in the constellation Hydra. This planet, known as 2M1207b, was imaged in 2005 by the European Southern Observatory's Very Large Telescope using an

In an artist's concept, an Earth-sized planet transits across the face of a sun-like main sequence star.

optics system called NaCo (short for Nasmyth Adaptive Optics System Near-Infrared Imager and Spectrograph). NaCo was equipped with visible light sensors and infrared heat sensors in addition to an infrared camera and spectrometer in order to accomplish the feat. Direct imaging continued to improve over the next decade, and now several large direct imaging projects are underway.

GEMINI PLANET IMAGER (GPI)

Perhaps the best-known direct imaging instrument is GPI: the Gemini Planet Imager. The difficulty with direct imaging is simple: the light of a star is so bright that it is almost impossible to pick out the tiny light given off by a planet in comparison to the star's light. Try to imagine picking out the light of a firefly circling a streetlight 1,000 miles away: distinguishing a planet from its parent star's light is even harder than that. Instruments like GPI solve this problem by using a telescope called a coronagraph, which can offer a view of objects very close to a star. The coronagraph uses a disc to block the star's bright light, basically producing an artificial solar eclipse while leaving the faint light of its planets visible. Unsurprisingly, instruments designed to achieve such a feat are built to what GPI's former systems engineer Leslie Saddlemyer describes as "excruciating" specificity. "Each individual mirror inside GPI has to be smooth to within a few times the size of an atom," Saddlemyer explained in a press release. This level of extreme precision allows GPI to view objects that are ten million times fainter than their host stars. Like NaCo before it, GPI provides spectroscopy of objects it observes, which lets it detect young, warm planets (up to about one billion years of age) through the infrared light they give off.

Direct imaging instruments like GPI are designed to get a good look at massive gas giants that have long orbital periods around their stars. Direct imaging is a much better method to observe these bodies than the transit method—a transit only lasts for a short amount of time, and a planet must make at least one full revolution around its star before another transit may be observed. GPI can see these bodies without having to wait for them to complete a full orbital period and will produce the first comprehensive survey of giant exoplanets that orbit in the same region giant planets exist in our solar system, far further out than the habitable zone where liquid water can exist.

Giant, long-orbiting exoplanets aren't the only thing these instruments can see: GPI tools can also measure the polarization of light to view very faint disks of dust from alien solar systems' comet and asteroid belts, like our own Milky Way's Kuiper Belt. GPI's first light (the very first astronomical image it took) showed light scattered by a disk of dust orbiting a young star called HR4796A. This sort of formation is called a circumstellar disk, which can offer another avenue of investigating planetary systems: planets can shape the disk into a ring shape around a star as they move along in their orbits. Observing the shape of circumstellar disks can help scientists learn about as-yet-undiscovered planets' orbits, and even learn about planetary formation in faraway systems. Around young stars, circumstellar disks provide material from which new planets may form. Seeing these around a mature star indicates that planets are probably present in its system, and a ring of dust around a white dwarf indicates that planets may still be present and continuing to orbit even though their star has died.

In this artwork, a huge dust ring orbits the massive star HR 4796A. One planet remains inside the dust boundary, another further away, around the edges of the ring.

A HEYDAY FOR DIRECT IMAGING

"The entire exoplanet community is excited for GPI to usher in a whole new era of planet finding," physicist and exoplanet expert Sara Seager of the Massachusetts Institute of Technology said in a press release on the Gemini Observatory's first light. "Each exoplanet detection technique has its heyday," Seager explained. "First it was the radial velocity technique (ground-based planet searches that started the whole field). Second it was the transit technique (namely

Kepler). Now it is the 'direct imaging' planet-finding technique's turn to make waves." Direct imaging is the latest tactic in the great exoplanet hunt, but that doesn't mean that other methods of planet detection have been rendered obsolete.

Evryscope, a transit-viewing instrument that began operations in 2015, sacrifices depth of view in order to be able to monitor the accessible sky— 1/4 of the the entire sky surrounding our Earth— all at once. With its 780 million-pixel detector, Evryscope records a continuous movie of the night sky in two-minute exposures in hopes of catching planetary transits in action. Its dome-shaped array of twenty-seven small telescopes (which inspired *Science* reporter Daniel Clery to write that it "looks more like an architectural folly than a telescope") also allows Evryscope to operate on a modest budget while yielding impressive results.

While other transit-observing missions like Kepler have focused on stars similar to our own sun, Evryscope's field of view allows it a chance to capture a transit around a white dwarf, a feat which—as of summer 2015—has yet to be

WHY CHILE?

You may have noticed that many of the ground-based telescopes mentioned in the hunt for exoplanets are located in Chile, regardless of each instrument's country of origin. Why do astronomers from all over the world travel to Chile to perform their observations? There are several reasons, according to a 2011 report from BBC News. The Latin American nation's clear desert skies are a primary draw, allowing for observations unobstructed by atmospheric interference. In some parts of the Atacama Desert, rainfall has never been recorded!

The La Silla Observatory in Chile's Atacama Desert offers a crystal clear view of the Southern Cross constellation.

Altitude is another consideration: the higher the telescope is located above sea level, in general, the better the view. Chile's Andes mountain range offers the equivalent of a front-row seat for observing the universe. Latitude is another factor. If you want to look at stars in the southern hemisphere, you can't install your telescope in Europe or North America. Additionally, Chile's stable government allows for investment in expensive long-term observational projects. By 2025, calculations project that Chile will serve as home to more than half of the image-capturing capacity in the entire world.

accomplished. White dwarves, old, burned-out remnants of stars, are only about the size of Earth. A planet crossing in front of a white dwarf might obscure the star completely as it passed but would do so very quickly, within perhaps two minutes. An exoplanet searcher would have to be looking in the exact right spot at the right time in order to notice the occurrence at all.

Evryscope's continuous monitoring allows its team to look at as much sky as possible in the hopes of observing it. The instrument's twenty-seven unsleeping eyes generate enough data to fill up more than 21,000 DVDs per year, and the project team is currently in discussion with observatories in different parts of the world in hopes of setting up more Evryscopes to observe the entire sky. PLATO (PLAnetary Transits and Oscillations of stars), a space-based observatory scheduled for launch by 2024, will use thirty-four small telescopes in order to map half of the sky and attempt to catch nearby exoplanets in transit.

OTHER METHODS FOR EXTRASOLAR AND EXOPLANETARY SEARCH

Radial velocity observations, the transit method, and direct imaging are the three primary techniques used to search for extrasolar systems, but they are not the only processes used to locate exoplanets. Astrometry, the oldest method used to infer the presence of extrasolar planets, measures the position of a star to see if it moves in response to an unseen orbital body. Interferometry collects light with mirrors and combines it to measure a star's movements very precisely. Microlensing measures spikes in the brightness of very faraway stars—hundreds of light-years away from Earth, near the center of the galaxy—in order to determine the presence of planets in their surrounding systems. A Starshade is a large flower-shaped structure flown in formation with a companion telescope that is shaped to control the diffraction of starlight for direct imaging of exoplanets.

New methods of utilizing old technology further the search for exoplanets as well. In April 2015, researchers used the HARPS radial velocity instrument to directly detect visible light reflected from the exoplanet 51 Pegasi b. "The team noted it was particularly interesting that the detection was possible with data collected by an existing observing facility," wrote Tushna Commissariat in an article for *Physics World*.

All existing exoplanet search methods are limited to basically that: locating exoplanets, and providing some information about their basic properties. As Jeff Foust wrote in a 2015 essay for the *Space Review*, "We don't know, however, if these or other Earth-like planets are really like the Earth in the characteristics that really count: whether they have atmospheres like the Earth, oceans of liquid water like the Earth, and life like the Earth. Those determinations are largely beyond the capabilities of ground- and space-based observatories in operation today. A new generation—arguably, generations—of instruments and telescopes will be needed to determine just how Earth-like these Earth-like worlds really are." As scientists continue to push the boundaries of existing technology, exoplanet science has nowhere to go but up.

CHAPTER FOUR

HOT JUPITERS, ICE GIANTS, AND SUPER-EARTHS: VARIETY IN THE UNIVERSE

The thousands of exoplanets in hundreds of alien solar systems discovered in the last two decades serve to demonstrate the huge variety of planetary systems across the galaxy. The hunt for extrasolar planets has revealed planetary types and behaviors that—based on data derived from our own solar system—scientists previously thought were impossible.

HOT JUPITERS

51 Pegasi b is a well-known exoplanet first discovered in 1995 using radial velocity observations. It is also an example of a hot Jupiter, a planetary type that does not exist within our

Exoplanet 51 Pegasi b, also known as Bellerophon, a hot Jupiter, was the first exoplanet discovered orbiting a main sequence star similar to our sun.

solar system. Like Jupiter, a hot Jupiter is a gas giant, but it orbits much closer to its host star than any of the gas giants in our local solar system, causing an extremely high surface temperature. Many of the first exoplanets discovered are hot Jupiters. Because they are so massive and orbit so close to their stars, they are ideal candidates for detection via the radial velocity method because their orbits quite obviously affect the motion of their respective stars.

Additionally, hot Jupiters can be seen to transit their stars relatively often, given their short orbital periods. Scientists believe that hot Jupiters form much farther away from their parent stars and then proceed to migrate to their later positions. A hot Jupiter has never yet been discovered orbiting a red giant star—a huge, cool star nearing the end of its lifespan. Our own Jupiter could potentially become a hot Jupiter when the sun becomes a red giant and expands far beyond its current size.

PUFFY PLANETS

Some hot Jupiters with very low density but a very large radius are known as puffy planets. These planets puff up to their large-seeming size due to the intense heat caused by proximity to their stars. Combined with internal greenhouse heating, puffy planets' atmospheres inflate to make them appear huge. A number of hot Jupiters have been found to have retrograde orbits, meaning they orbit in the opposite direction of their stars' rotation. Some scientists think that these backward-orbiting planets owe their rotational direction to gravitational interactions with other bodies as they migrated inward toward their current positions close to their host stars. Others, however, think that the stars hosting these retrograde exoplanets may have actually flipped over at some point during the planetary formation process, influenced by interaction with a surrounding ring of planet-forming dust and debris. Perhaps both ideas are valid. Continued research should shed light on the mystery.

ICE GIANTS

Unlike close-orbiting gas giants, ice giants such as Uranus and Neptune are thought to have formed closer to their stars than their present positions and then migrated outward. "Maybe you need some kind of jostling to make planets like Uranus and Neptune," remarked professor Andrew Gould of Ohio State University. Discovery of the first extrasolar ice giant was confirmed in 2010 through the gravitational microlensing process. This particular planet lies more than 25,000 light

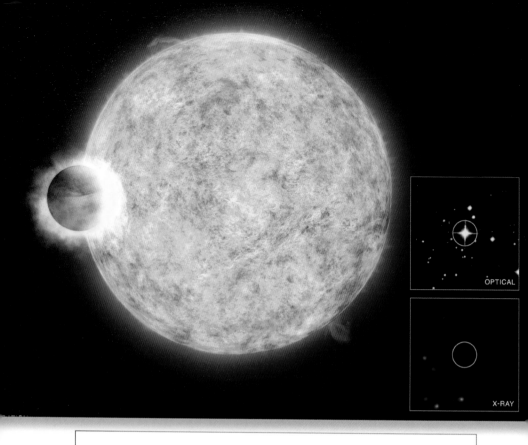

OPTICAL

X-RAY

Hot Jupiters and ice giants showcase the extraordinary amount of variety in solar systems across the galaxy.

years away from our own position in the galaxy, and leads an odd orbital life: it revolves around one star in a binary star system, passing so close to the second star that its orbital path is affected by the second star's gravity. Despite these unfamiliar circumstances, scientists imagine that it is something of an analog for our own solar system's Uranus.

The Kepler space observatory spotted the first rocky, Earth-size planet found outside our solar system in late 2013. Unlike Earth, Kepler-78b does not reside within the habitable zone of its system but orbits very close to its star, transiting between the star and Kepler every 8.5 hours. Measurements of the size and mass of Kepler-78b indicate that it may be made primarily of rock and iron.

In summer 2015, data provided by NASA's Spitzer Space Telescope confirmed the presence of the closest rocky planet discovered outside our solar system yet. Like Kepler-78b, HD 219134b orbits much too close to its star to sustain life. However, its proximity to Earth and frequent transiting schedule makes it a perfect candidate for continued research. "Most of the known planets are hundreds of light-years away. This one is practically a next-door neighbor," astronomer Lars A. Buchhave told CNN of the find. HD 219134b is a super-Earth, a rocky planet with bigger-than-Earth proportions, and offers one of the first chances to study such a specimen in detail.

Thanks to the Kepler mission, we know that many super-Earths exist in the galaxy but do not know very much about them. HD 219134b "can be considered a kind of Rosetta Stone for the study of super-Earths," said Michael Gillon, lead scientist on the Spitzer detection of the planet's transit.

55 CANCRI E: A DIAMOND GIANT?

Another super-Earth located about forty light-years from our solar system, 55 Cancri e, has long been thought to consist primarily of diamond—a literal giant diamond in the sky. Research suggested that the eight-times-more-massive-than-Earth diamond planet has a surface of graphite surrounding a thick layer of diamond, rather than Earth's more pedestrian (but life-sustaining) water and granite. New research on the composition of the planet's host star, however, indicates that it might not be so sparkling as scientists initially thought.

New exoplanet discoveries continue to reveal planetary compositions and circumstances that scientists previously assumed impossible based on observations of our own solar system.

Room for uncertainty remains, however. "We still don't know whether our solar system is common or uncommon in the universe because many of the systems that we are finding have giant gas planets closer to the star, unlike our system where rocky planets dominate the inner orbits and gas giants occur further out," said Johanna Teske of the University of Arizona to the

The atmosphere of 55 Cancri e is imagined in this illustration. As much as 30 percent of the planet may be carbon in the form of diamond.

University of Arizona News. "But based on what we know at this point, 55 Cancri e is more of a 'diamond in the rough.'"

In May 2015, 55 Cancri e made news when scientists using NASA's Spitzer Space Telescope observed something remarkable: between 2011 and 2013, the planet's temperatures swung between 1,000 to 2,700 degrees Celsius, or 1,832 to 4,892 degrees Fahrenheit. This was the first time a signature of thermal emissions had ever been detected for a super-Earth. Researchers don't yet know what caused the extreme temperature shift, but they suspect it might indicate volcanic activity on the planet's surface spewing out huge amounts of gas and dust into the atmosphere. The temperature shift occurred on the "day side" of 55 Cancri e (because the planet is tidally locked so one side always faces its star and the other faces away, it doesn't experience a day and night cycle the way Earth's inhabitants do). If 55 Cancri e's massive temperature variability is indeed caused by volcanic activity, then it is more volcanic than any body that exists in our solar system.

KEPLER 138B

In June 2015, the first exoplanet smaller than Earth in mass and size was measured. Like many Earth-size and super-Earth exoplanets, Kepler 138b is most likely far too hot to be habitable, but it is an exciting find nonetheless. "Kepler-138b is roughly 3,000 times less massive than the first exoplanet whose density was measured 15 years ago," Eric Ford, professor of astronomy and astrophysics at Penn State University, said on his university's website. "We now are working to discover and characterize rocky planets in the habitable zones of nearby stars."

In order to refine the hunt for Goldilocks worlds, two teams at the Harvard-Smithsonian Center for Astrophysics have done theoretical work to calculate the sizes and masses of planets most likely to be friendly to life as we know it. These scientists have found that smaller worlds less than 1.6 times Earth's size tend to have the right masses to be made from the same rocky materials as Earth. "Our solar system is not as unique as we might have thought. It looks like rocky exoplanets use the same basic ingredients," Kepler scientist Douglas Caldwell told Smithsonian.com. Larger super-Earths between two and four times the mass of our planet seem best for building and maintaining stable oceans to support carbon-based life. Calculations show that such a world would take approximately a billion years to develop an ocean. "Assuming evolution follows a similar rate as it has on Earth, our best bet for finding a planet with life may be a super-Earth that's at

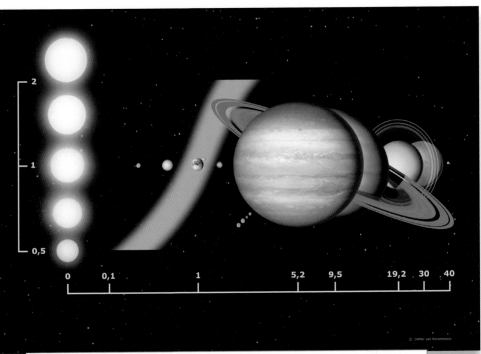

Though solar systems across the galaxy may be very different from one another, all planets are made from the same elemental building blocks found within our local solar system.

least 5.5 billion years old," noted Smithsonian reporter Victoria Jaggard.

ANOTHER EARTH IN A GOLDILOCKS ZONE?

In July 2015 scientists announced the discovery of Kepler-455b, which possesses more Earth-like traits than any exoplanet yet located. Based on its size—about 60 percent bigger than

THE SEARCH FOR EXTRATERRESTRIAL LIFE

In spring 2015, spurred by recent exciting exoplanet-related findings, NASA announced a huge cooperative effort to analyze other worlds for possible life: the Nexus for Exoplanet System Science (NExSS for short). This marks the first time NASA has funded an effort to locate extraterrestrial life since the High Resolution Microwave Survey to search for extraterrestrial transmissions was initiated in 1992 and defunded by Congress less than a year later. The project will combine the efforts of many different scientists in order to better understand exoplanets and search for biosignatures (signs of life) by applying system science—studying the way biology interacts with the atmosphere, geology, oceans, and interior of a planet, and the way all of these elements are affected by the planet's host star. Earth scientists will study our own planet in order to develop a systems science approach; and planetary scientists will apply systems science to other worlds within our solar system. Heliophysicists who study our sun will provide information about how our local star interacts with orbiting planets, and astrophysicists will provide new data on exoplanets and their host stars for future study. This unprecedented grouping of research communities will work together to classify the different worlds discovered, research the potential habitability of these planets, and develop new tools and technologies in order to search for life elsewhere in the galaxy.

Earth and possibly five times as massive—Kepler-452b might not sound much like Earth, but its 385-day orbit around a sun-like G2-class star places it firmly within a carbon-based habitable zone where liquid water could potentially exist. No previously discovered "Goldilocks zone" planets are both relatively close to Earth in size and

A "travel poster" created by NASA's Jet Propulsion Laboratory shows the two suns a visitor standing on the surface of Kepler-16b would see in the sky.

also orbit a sun-like star. The planet's host star Kepler-452 is about 1.5 billion years older than the sun, and Kepler-425b has possibly been orbiting inside the star's habitable zone for six billion years. At this point researchers have not been able to learn whether Kepler-452b has a rocky surface like Earth's. As it lies 1,400 light-years away from Earth, we will have to develop more advanced technology than presently available in order to find out.

Some exoplanets are circumbinary planets, meaning they circle two stars instead of one. If a human could stand on the surface of such a planet, they would see two suns in the sky instead of one. Kepler-453b, announced in August 2015, is one such planet: its orbital distance puts it within the habitable zone of its stars. However, as Kepler-453b is most likely a gas giant with a radius more than six times greater than that of Earth, it probably does not serve as home to any lifeforms similar to those that live on the third planet from the sun. Researchers were lucky to detect a transit when Kepler-453b crossed between its stars and the Kepler space observatory, and if they had missed this crossing they wouldn't have another chance to catch the planet in transit until 2066. "If we had observed this planet earlier or later than we

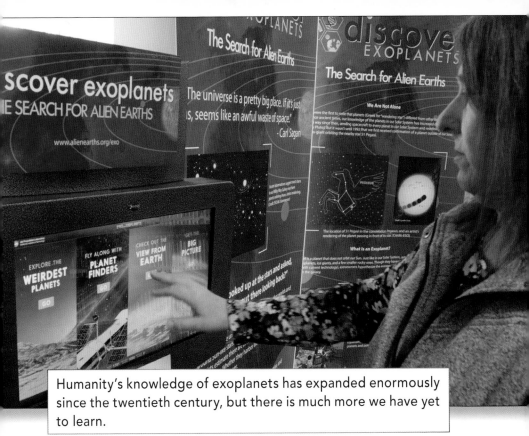

Humanity's knowledge of exoplanets has expanded enormously since the twentieth century, but there is much more we have yet to learn.

did, we would have seen nothing and assumed there was no planet there," said Stephen Kane, one of the team members who made the discovery. "That suggests that there are a lot more of these kinds of planets than we are thinking, and we're just looking at the wrong time."

The modern history of exoplanet discovery is just beginning, with those first confirmed discovered by Wolszczan and Dale Frail in only 1992. By 2015, previously unimaginable varieties of exoplanets and planetary systems

GLIESE 581 C

Gliese 581 c was discovered by the Swiss astronomer Stephane Udry and his team on April 4, 2007. This was the second planet discovered orbiting the red dwarf Gliese 581, and it is third in orbit from its star. It is classified as a super-Earth and has a mass at least 5.5 times that of Earth itself.

Gliese 581 c first excited researchers due to its distance from its star, which made them believe that

A very small planet—possibly the smallest yet located outside of our own solar system—orbits the dwarf star Gliese 581 in the constellation Libra.

it could possibly support an atmosphere where liquid water was possible. Further research dispelled these notions and indicated that Gliese 581 c probably lies just outside the habitable zone. It most likely resembles Venus in its atmospheric conditions. Two years after its discovery, another planet in its system, Gliese 581 e, was discovered, which boasts 1.9 Earth masses.

Gliese 581 c, which orbits within the Goldilocks zone of its star, may be the most Earth-like exoplanet yet located.

have been discovered, and scientists are just getting started. As the development of new technology and research methods allow exoplanet searchers to view more of the sky continuously and to view sights in the cosmos at ever greater distances, they will surely discover even more planetary phenomena as yet undreamed. Scientists will continue to discover, catalogue, and study the properties of extrasolar planets. Humanity, in turn, will likely find that the galaxy is an even more diverse and incredible place than we had ever suspected.

GLOSSARY

ASTROMETRY The oldest method used to infer the presence of extrasolar planets, astrometry measures the position of a star to see if it moves in response to an unseen orbital body.

BIOSIGNATURES Quantifiable signs of biological life.

BROWN DWARF A small star-mass object equal to or larger than approximately thirteen Jupiter masses, big enough to fuse deuterium in its core.

CELESTIAL Positioned in or relating to the sky, or outer space as observed in astronomy.

CIRCUMBINARY PLANET A planet that orbits two stars, rather than one.

CIRCUMSTELLAR DISK A ring of dust orbiting a star.

DIRECT IMAGING Method that allows an exoplanet to be viewed directly by measuring light reflected by the planet or thermal infrared radiation emitted by the planet and discounting the overwhelming light of the planet's parent star.

FIRST LIGHT The first time a new telescope or new instrument is used to take an astronomical image.

HABITABLE ZONE Also known as the "Goldilocks zone," the range of distance surrounding a star in which liquid water can exist on a planet's surface.

HOT JUPITER Gas giant that orbits very close to its star, causing extremely high surface temperatures.

ICE GIANT Large planet composed primarily of ice, such as Neptune and Uranus.

INTERFEROMETRY A method of collecting light with mirrors and combining it to measure a star's movements very precisely.

MICROLENSING Method of measuring spikes in the brightness of very faraway stars in order to determine the presence of planets in their systems.

ORBIT The revolution of celestial bodies around one another due to the force of gravity.

ORBITAL PERIOD The amount of time it takes an orbiting body to make one full revolution around the object that it orbits.

RADIAL VELOCITY METHOD A way of locating exoplanets by using a spectrograph to measure shifts in a star's light spectrum as it moves toward and away from Earth in response to the movement of orbiting bodies. Also called "Doppler spectroscopy."

RETROGRADE ORBIT An orbit that moves in opposition to the rotation of the object it revolves around.

STARSHADE A large flower-shaped structure flown in formation with a companion telescope that is shaped to control the diffraction of starlight for direct imaging of exoplanets.

STELLAR Of or relating to a star or stars.

SUPER-EARTH A planet with more mass than that of Earth but less than a giant planet such as Neptune.

SYSTEM SCIENCE The study of the way a planet's physical features and biology interact with one another and are affected by the planet's host star.

THERMONUCLEAR FUSION A way to

achieve nuclear fusion through extremely high temperatures, occurs in the cores of stars.

TRANSIT PHOTOMETRY Technique that measures drops in starlight caused by planets that pass between their parent stars and the telescope in order to determine the planet's size and orbital period.

FOR MORE INFORMATION

American Astronomical Society
2000 Florida Avenue NW, Suite 400
Washington, DC 20009
Website: http://aas.org
The American Astronomical Society is the
    major organization of professional astrono-
    mers in North America.

National Aeronautics and Space
    Administration (NASA)
300 E Street SW
Washington, DC 20546
(202) 358-0001
Website: http://www.nasa.gov
The National Aeronautics and Space Adminis-
    tration (NASA) is the United States' federal
    government agency responsible for the civil-
    ian space program and aeronautics and aero-
    space research.

The Planetary Society
60 South Los Robles Avenue
Pasadena, CA 91101
(626) 793-5100

Website: http://planetary.org
The Planetary Society is a nonprofit, nongovern-
    mental organization dedicated to exploration
    of the solar system and the universe at large,
    and extraterrestrial life, with membership
    open to anyone.

Royal Astronomical Society of Canada
4920 Dundas Street West
Etobicoke, ON M9A 1B7
Canada
Website: http://rascto.ca
The Royal Astronomical Society of Canada is
    Canada's largest astronomy organization.

The SETI League, Inc.
433 Liberty Street
Little Ferry, NJ 07643ff
(201) 641-1770
Website: http://www.setileague.org
SETI (Search for Extra-Terrestrial Intelligence) is a
    grassroots organization of amateur and pro-
    fessional radio astronomers with 1,500 mem-
    bers in sixty-two nations.

SkyNews
425 Adelaide Street West
Toronto, ON M5V 3C1
Canada
Website: http://www.skynews.ca
The Canadian magazine *SkyNews* provides
   its readers with coverage of astronomy and
   stargazing.

WEBSITES

Because of the changing number of Internet links,
Rosen Publishing has developed an online list of
websites related to the subject of this book. This
site is updated regularly. Please use this link to
access the list:

http://www.rosenlinks.com/SOE/Find

FOR FURTHER READING

Billings, Lee. *Five Billion Years of Solitude: The Search for Life Among the Stars*. New York, NY: Penguin Group, 2013.

Chown, Marcus. *Solar System: A Visual Exploration of All the Planets, Moons and Other Heavenly Bodies that Orbit Our Sun*. New York, NY: Black Dog & Leventhal Publishers, Inc., 2011.

Dinwiddie, Robert, et al. *The Planets*. New York, NY: DK, 2014.

Encrenaz, Therese. *Planets: Ours and Others: From Earth to Exoplanets*. Hackensack, NJ: World Scientific Publishing Co., 2013.

Geach, James. *Galaxy: Mapping the Cosmos*. London, England: Reaktion Books Ltd., 2014.

Kops, Deborah. *Exploring Exoplanets*. Minneapolis, MN: Lerner Publications, 2013.

Mo, Houjun, et al. *Galaxy Formation and Evolution*. Cambridge, England: Cambridge University Press, 2010.

Perryman, Michael. *The Exoplanet Handbook*. Cambridge, England: Cambridge University Press, 2014.

Pont, Frédéric J. *Alien Skies: Planetary Atmospheres from Earth to Exoplanets*. New York, NY: Springer, 2014.

Rothery, David. *Planets: A Very Short Introduction*. Oxford, England: Oxford University Press, 2010.

Scharf, Caleb. *The Copernicus Complex: Our Cosmic Significance in a Universe of Planets and Probabilities*. New York, NY: Scientific American, 2014.

Scientific American Editors. *Exoplanets: Worlds Without End*. New York, NY: Scientific American, 2015.

Seager, Sarah. *Exoplanet Atmospheres: Physical Processes*. Princeton, NJ: Princeton University Press, 2010.

Seeds, Michael, and Dana Backman. *The Solar System*. Pacific Grove, CA: Brooks Cole, 2015.

Sengupta, Sujan. *Worlds Beyond Our Own: The Search for Habitable Planets*. Bangalore, India: Springer, 2014.

Simon, Seymour. *Galaxies*. New York, NY: Harper Collins, 1991.

Stott, Carole, and David Hughes. *Solar System*.

Edison, NJ: Sterling, 2013.

Tyson, Neil deGrasse, and Donald Goldsmith. *Origins: Fourteen Billion Years of Cosmic Evolution*. New York, NY: W. W. Norton & Company, Inc., 2004.

U.S. Government. *Complete Guide to the Kepler Space Telescope Mission and the Search for Habitable Planets and Earth-like Exoplanets - Planet Detection Strategies, Mission History and Accomplishments*. Progressive Management: 2013.

Yaqoob, Tahir. *Exoplanets and Alien Solar Systems*. Baltimore, MD: New Earth Labs (Education and Outreach), 2011.

BIBLIOGRAPHY

Astronomy.com. "Diamond 'Super-Earth' May Not Be Quite as Precious as Once Thought." October 9, 2013. Retrieved August 10, 2015 (http://www.astronomy.com/news/2013/10/diamond-super-earth-may-not-be-quite-as-precious-as-once-thought).

Barnett, Amanda. "Nearest Rocky Planet Outside of Solar System Found." CNN News, July 30, 2015. Retrieved August 10, 2015 (http://www.cnn.com/2015/07/30/us/exoplanet-discovered).

Chang, Kenneth. "Puzzling Puffy Planet, Less Dense Than Cork, Is Discovered." *New York Times*, September 16, 2006. Retrieved August 10, 2015 (http://www.nytimes.com/2006/09/15/science/space/15planet.html?_r=0).

Clery, Daniel. "Small Scopes Log an Ever-changing Sky." *Science*, July 3, 2015. Retrieved August 10, 2015 (http://www.sciencemag.org/content/349/6243/14.full).

Commissariat, Tushna. "First Visible Light Detected Directly from an Exoplanet." *Physics World*, April 22, 2015. Retrieved

August 20, 2015 (http://physicsworld.com/cws/article/news/2015/apr/22/first-visible-light-detected-directly-from-an-exoplanet).

European Southern Observatory. "NaCo Nasmyth Adaptive Optics System (NAOS) Near-Infrared Imager and Spectrograph (CONICA)." Retrieved August 10, 2015 (http://www.eso.org/sci/facilities/paranal/instruments/naco.html).

European Southern Observatory Observation Report. "2M1207b - First Image of an Exoplanet." Retrieved August 10, 2015 (http://www.eso.org/public/usa/images/26a_big-vlt).

European Southern Observatory Press Release. "First Light for SPHERE Exoplanet Imager: Revolutionary New VLT instrument Installed." June 4, 2014. Retrieved August 10, 2015 (http://www.eso.org/public/usa/news/eso1417/).

European Southern Observatory Press Release. "New Exoplanet-hunting Telescopes on Paranal: NGTS Facility Achieves First Light." January 14, 2015. Retrieved August 10,

2015 (http://www.eso.org/public/usa/news/
eso1502/).

European Space Agency Press Release. "ESA
Selects Planet-Hunting PLATO Mission."
February 19, 2014. Retrieved August 20,
2015 (http://sci.esa.int/plato/53707-esa-
selects-planet-hunting-plato-mission).

Extrasolar Planets Encyclopaedia. "Extrasolar Planets Global Searches (Ongoing Pro-
grammes and Future Projects)." Retrieved
August 10, 2015 (http://exoplanet.eu/
research).

Feltman, Rachel. "Newly Discovered Exoplanet
Orbits a Pair of Stars." *Washington Post*,
August 10, 2015. Retrieved August 20, 2015
(http://www.washingtonpost.com/
news/speaking-of-science/wp/2015/08/10/
newly-discovered-exoplanet-or-
bits-a-pair-of-stars).

Foust, Jeff. "Debating the Future of Exoplanet
Missions Concepts and Community." *Space
Review*, January 19, 2015. Retrieved August
20, 2015 (http://www.thespacereview.com/
article/2679/1).

Gemini Observatory Press Release. "Gemini Planet Imager First Light!" January 7, 2014. Retrieved August 10, 2015 (http://www.gemini.edu/node/12113).

Gemini Planet Imager Exoplanet Survey: Imaging and Characterizing Exoplanets. Retrieved August 10, 2015 (http://planetimager.org).

Gorder, Pam Frost. "Astronomers Spot Far-away Uranus-Like Planet." Ohio State University, October 15, 2014. Retrieved August 10, 2015 (https://news.osu.edu/news/2014/10/15/astronomers-spot-faraway-uranus-like-planet).

International Astronomical Union. "IAU 2006 General Assembly: Result of the IAU Resolution Votes." August 24, 2006. Retrieved August 10, 2015 (http://www.iau.org/news/pressreleases/detail/iau0603/).

International Astronomical Union. "Naming of Exoplanets." 2015. Retrieved August 20, 2015 (https://www.iau.org/public/themes/naming_exoplanets).

Jacob, Capt. W. S. "On Certain Anomalies Pre-

sented by the Binary Star 70 Ophiuchi."
Monthly Notices of the Royal Astronomical Society, Vol. XV. Nov. 1854–June 1855.
Retrieved August 10, 2015 (https://play.google.com/books/reader?id=pQsAAAAAMAAJ&printsec=frontcover&output=reader&hl=en).

Jaggard, Victoria. "New Super-Earths Double the Number of Life-Friendly Worlds." *Smithsonian Magazine*, January 6, 2015. Retrieved August 20, 2015 (http://www.smithsonianmag.com/science-nature/new-super-earths-discovered-oceans-life-exoplanets-180953805/?no-ist).

Jet Propulsion Laboratory, California Institute of Technology."NASA's Spitzer Confirms Closest Rocky Exoplanet." July 30, 2015. Retrieved August 10, 2015 (http://www.jpl.nasa.gov/news/news.php?feature=4672).

Johnson, Michele (page ed.). "How Many Exoplanets Has Kepler Discovered?" NASA, June 5, 2015. Retrieved August 10, 2015 (http://www.nasa.gov/kepler/discoveries).

Loff, Sarah. "NASA's NExSS Coalition to Lead

Search for Life on Distant Worlds." NASA, April 21, 2015. Retrieved August 10, 2015 (https://www.nasa.gov/feature/nasa-s-nexss-coalition-to-lead-search-for-life-on-distant-worlds).

Long, Gideon. "Why Chile Is an Astronomer's Paradise." BBC News, July 25, 2011. Retrieved August 10, 2015 (http://www.bbc.com/news/world-latin-america-14205720).

Major, Jason. "Super-sensitive Camera Captures a Direct Image of an Exoplanet." *Universe Today*, January 7, 2014. Retrieved August 10, 2015 (http://www.universetoday.com/107854/super-sensitive-camera-captures-a-direct-image-of-an-exoplanet).

O'Neill, Ian. "Kepler-452b: The Closest Exoplanet Match to Earth." *Discovery News*, July 23, 2015. Retrieved August 10, 2015 (http://news.discovery.com/space/alien-life-exoplanets/kepler-452b--the-closest-exoplanet-match-to-earth-150723.htm).

Overbye, Dennis. "Two Earth-Size Planets Are Discovered." *New York Times*, December 20, 2011. Retrieved August 20, 2015 (http://www.nytimes.com/2011/12/21/science/space/nasas-kepler-spacecraft-discovers-2-earth-size-planets.html).

Penn State Science. "A First: Exoplanet Smaller than Earth Gets Its Size and Mass Measured." June 16, 2015. Retrieved August 10, 2015 (http://science.psu.edu/news-and-events/2015-news/Ford6-2015).

The Planetary Society. "Radial Velocity: The First Method that Worked." Retrieved July 1, 2015 (http://www.planetary.org/explore/space-topics/exoplanets/radial-velocity.html).

Royal Astronomical Society Press Release. "Turning Planetary Theory Upside Down." April 12, 2010. Retrieved August 10, 2015 (http://www.astro.gla.ac.uk/nam2010/pr10.php).

Stevenson, David. *Under a Crimson Sun: Prospects for Life in a Red Dwarf System.*

New York, NY: Springer Science+Business Media, 2013.

Thomson, Mark, et al. "Starshade Update: August Was a Month of 'Discovery' for Starshade Technology." *Exoplanet Exploration Program Newsletter*, October 2013. Retrieved August 10, 2015 (http://exep.jpl.nasa.gov/newsletters/issue12/starshade).

University of Geneva, Astronomy Department. "HARPS: High Accuracy Radial Velocity Planetary Search Project." 2015. Retrieved August 20, 2015 (http://exoplanets.ch/projects/harps).

Wall, Mike. "Alien Volcanoes on 'Super Earth' May Explain Wild Temperature Swings." Space.com, May 5, 2015. Retrieved August 20, 2015 (http://www.space.com/29303-super-earth-volcanoes-planet-55-cancri-e.html).

W. M. Keck Observatory. "First Earth-Sized, Rocky Exoplanet Found." October 30, 2013. Retrieved August 10, 2015 (http://www.keckobservatory.org/recent/entry/

first_earth_sized_rocky_exoplanet_found).

Working Group on Extrasolar Planets of the International Astronomical Union. "Position Statement on the Definition of a 'Planet.'" February 28, 2003. Retrieved August 10, 2015 (http://w.astro.berkeley. edu/~basri/defineplanet/IAU-WGExSP. htm).

Young, Monica. "The Future of Exoplanet Hunts." Sky & Telescope: The Essential Guide to Astronomy. Retrieved August 20, 2015 (http://www.skyandtelescope. com/astronomy-news/future-exoplanet-hunts-01202015).

INDEX

A

Almagest, 9
Apollonius of Perga, 9
Aristarchus of Samos,
    9–11
astrometry, 67

B

brown dwarf stars, 26,
    39, 47
Bruno, Giordano, 11
Buchhave, Lars A., 75

C

Caldwell, Douglas, 80
Campbell, Bruce, 19, 24,
    44
Chile, as place for astro-
    nomical observations,
    65–66
circumbinary planet,
    explanation of, 84
circumstellar disk, expla-
    nation of, 61
Clery, Daniel, 64
Commissariat, Tushna, 68
Copernicus, Nicolaus, 11
coronagraph, 59

D

Doppler spectroscopy,
    44–49

E

Evryscope, 40–41, 64–67
exoplanet, definition of, 6
exoplanets, naming of, 27

F

51 Pegasi, 26
51 Pegasi b, 70
55 Cancri e, 76–79
Ford, Eric, 79
Foust, Jeff, 68–69
Frail, Dale, 21–24, 44, 85

G

Galileo Galilei, 11–12
gas giants, 28
Gemini Planet Imager
    (GPI), 34–40, 59–61,
    63
Gillon, Michael, 76
Gliese 581 c, 86–87
Goldilocks zone, explana-
    tion of, 30
Gould, Andrew, 73

V
Venus, 15, 30, 87

W
Walker, G. A. H., 19, 24,
    44
Wolszczan, Aleksander,
    21–24, 44, 85

Y
Yang, Stephenson, 19, 24,
    44

ABOUT THE AUTHOR

Jennifer Culp is a medical editor and author of nonfiction science and tech books for children and young adults.

PHOTO CREDITS

Cover, p. 1 NASA/Getty Images; pp. 4-5, 50-51 David Ducros/Science Source; pp. 10, 76-77 Science Source; p. 12 Jay Pasachoff/SuperStock; p. 15 Babak Tafreshi/Science Source/Getty Images; pp. 17, 35, 62-63 Lynette Cook/ Science Source; pp. 18-19, 78 © Science Photo Library/ Alamy; pp. 22-23 Tim Draper/Dorling Kindersley/Getty Images; p. 25 Lionel Flusin/Gamma-Rapho/Getty Images; p. 29 Encyclopaedia Britannica/Universal Images Group/ Getty Images; pp. 32-33 Detlev van Ravenswaay/Picture Press/Getty Images; p. 37 © Richard Wainscoat/Alamy; p. 39 Sven Creutzmann/Mambo Photo/Hulton Archive/Getty Images; pp. 44-45, 58-59 Stocktrek Images/Getty Images; p. 49 © D Hale-Sutton/Alamy; pp. 54-55 Mark Garlick/Science Photo Library/Getty Images; p. 65 Babak Tafreshi/ National Geographic Image Collection/Getty Images; p. 71 Stocktrek Images/Kevin Lafin/Getty Images; p. 74 © NG Images/Alamy; p. 81 Detlev van Ravenswaay/Science Source; p. 83 NASA JPL/Rex Features/AP Images; p. 85 © AP Images; p. 86 MCT/Tribune News Service/Getty Images; p. 87 David A. Hardy/Science Source; interior pages background images (space) Yuriy Kulik/ Shutterstock.com, (light) Santiago Cornejo/Shutterstock.com; back cover Anatolii Vasilev/Shutterstock.com
Designer: Brian Garvey; Editor/Photo Researcher: Philip Wolny